The Mayflower

Susan Whitehurst

The Library
of the
PILGRIMS

The Rosen Publishing Group's
PowerKids Press™
New York

For the Lairds and the San Francisco Summer of 2000

Published in 2002 by The Rosen Publishing Group, Inc.
29 East 21st Street, New York, NY 10010

First Edition

Book Design: Maria E. Melendez

Project Editor: Frances E. Ruffin

Photo Credits: Cover and title page, the Mayflower departs and leaves the pilgrims, the signing of the Mayflower Compact, p. 4 (Pilgrims seeing the Mayflower departing), p. 7 (the pilgrims praying), p. 12 (the Mayflower ship), p. 17 (the Mayflower ship). © Bettmann/CORBIS; Cover and title page, the Mayflower ship, p. 4 (the Mayflower ship sailing) © AKG Photo London; p. 8 (Seventeenth century delft plate), p. 19 (workman's felt hat and shears for cutting cloth) © Museum of London; p. 8 (an oak cradle, Seventeenth century, 40 inches wide, 27 inches high, 24 inches deep), (an oak chest, early eighteenth century, 37 ½ inches wide, 54 ¼ inches high, 21 inches deep) © CHRISTIE'S IMAGES LTD; p. 8 (embroidered jacket worn by Margaret Laton, English, 1610-1620) © Victoria and Albert Museum; p. 4 (102 Protestants leave Plymouth for America in the Mayflower), p. 16 (apothecaries preparing medicines), p. 19 (a weaver), (a shoemaker) © Mary Evans Picture Library; pp. 10-11 (cross section of the Mayflower) © The Art Archive; p. 13 (pilgrims departing Delft Haven, Netherlands, 1620, Mayflower), p. 20 (pilgrims' farewell meeting on the Mayflower in 1620), p. 20 (the Mayflower at sea), p. 21 (Plymouth Rock, with Mayflower at anchor), p. 22 (signing the Mayflower Compact) © North Wind Pictures.

Whitehurst, Susan.
    The Mayflower / Susan Whitehurst.—
1st ed.
        p. cm. — (The library of the Pilgrims)
Includes index.
    ISBN 0-8239-5806-X
    1. Mayflower (Ship)—Juvenile literature. 2. Pilgrims (New Plymouth Colony)—Juvenile literature. 3.   Cape Cod (Mass.)—History—17th century—Juvenile literature. 4.   Massachusetts—History—New Plymouth, 1620-1691—Juvenile literature.   [1. Pilgrims (New Plymouth Colony)
    2. Mayflower (Ship) 3. Massachusetts—History—New Plymouth, 1620-1691.] I. Title.
    F68 .W59 2002
    974.4'8202—dc21

00-012308

Manufactured in the United States of America

Contents

The Mayflower stayed in Cape Cod for six months.

The Pilgrims landed in Cape Cod, an area in what later became the state of Massachusetts.

The Pilgrims: Saints and Strangers

A ship named the *Mayflower* sat in the harbor at Plymouth, England, on September 6, 1620. The ship was waiting for warm winds to fill its sails to begin a long trip to America. There would be 102 passengers, including 35 people known as the **Separatists**. They wanted to separate from the Church of England. They called themselves the Saints. There were 67 farmers and **tradesmen** and their families on the *Mayflower*. They hoped to find new opportunites in America. The Saints called them the Strangers. Thirty sailors also would make the trip to America.

All of the passengers on the *Mayflower* that day were people we know as the Pilgrims. Among them was Giles Hopkins, a 13-year-old boy who was lucky to be traveling with his whole family. There were 34 children to sail, but some of the passengers had to leave their younger children in England. The journey to America could be dangerous.

The *Mayflower* ship carried the Pilgrims to America.

Paying for the Journey

The Saints needed money to buy food and supplies for the journey to America. A group of English businessmen offered to pay for the trip. The Saints agreed to work for them for seven years. They had to ship furs, fish, and **timber** back to England for the businessmen to sell. The Saints bought a small ship, the *Speedwell*. To make sure the new **settlement** would be successful, the businessmen included farmers and tradesmen. They rented the *Mayflower* for their voyage. The *Mayflower* and the *Speedwell* first set sail on August 5, 1620.

When the Mayflower departed from England, the Saints prayed for their safety during the long voyage.

The Speedwell leaked so badly, that both ships had to return to England. They decided that the Speedwell was not safe and could not cross the ocean. One month later, the Saints, Strangers, and sailors all crowded into the Mayflower for the journey to America. The Mayflower was on her own. It was dangerous for a ship to sail alone. Usually two or three ships sailed together. There would be help if a ship ran into storms or ran out of food and water.

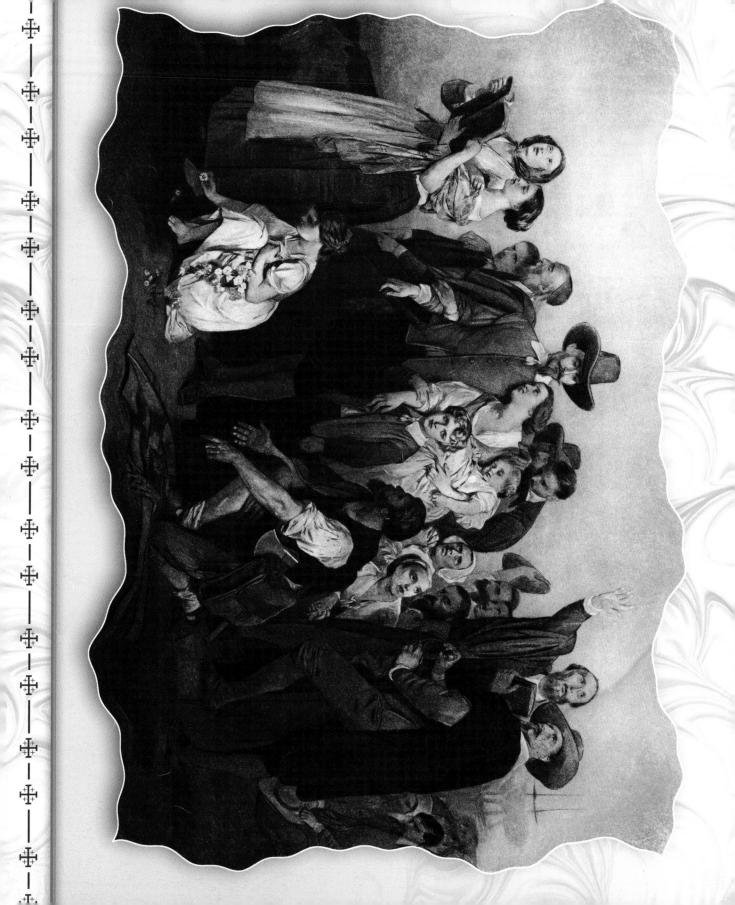

baby's cradle, chest

clothing that might have been packed by a Mayflower passenger

plate

Packing for a New Life

Giles Hopkins and his family could only bring one large chest, a Bible box, and a baby cradle. The chest had to contain everything they would need to **survive** in America. Giles and his father would need to hunt for food, so they packed knives, a **musket**, gunpowder, and fishing lines and hooks. Giles's mother, Elizabeth, would have put in pots and pans for cooking, as well as blankets and warm clothing. Every family would have to build their new home and plant a garden when they got to America.

The Pilgrims needed to raise farm animals when they got to America. They brought rabbits, chickens, geese, ducks, pigs, goats, and sheep. They also packed tools such as hammers and shovels for building houses. The Pilgrims had to be careful. There were no shops in America. What they carried on the Mayflower could mean the difference between life and death.

▲ People on the Mayflower brought things that they would need for their new lives in America.

Life Between Decks

The Mayflower was a good, sturdy ship. It had been used to carry wine, salt, vinegar, cloth, and hemp, which is a kind of rope. It was not set up to carry passengers, and certainly not 102 of them. This sailing ship was 90 feet (27.4 m) long and 26 feet (7.9 m) wide. It was as long as three school buses and as wide as one bus. The Pilgrims stayed on the 'tween **decks**, a level that was between the main deck on top and the hold below, where food, water, and baggage were stored. The ceiling there was only 5 feet (1.5 m) high. Young people like Giles could stand up, but adults had to bend over to walk.

This is a cross section of the Mayflower and the decks where people lived and worked during their voyage to the New World.

Children and young people were given a space about the size of a twin bed where they could eat, sleep, read, and play. At night they slept on the floor. There was little fresh air, and even less light on the 'tween decks.

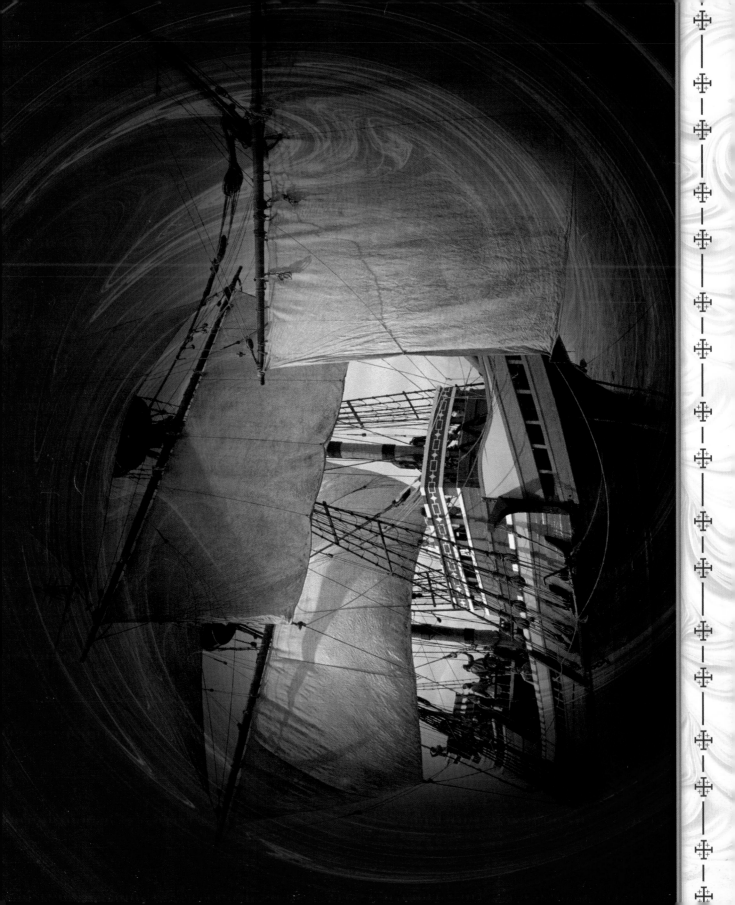

Wet and Cold

The weather had been warm and sunny when the Pilgrims left Plymouth, England, in September 1620. Once at sea, the *Mayflower* soon ran into terrible storms. The winds howled and the seas tossed the *Mayflower* around like a toy boat. The salty seawater soaked the main deck and dripped on the Pilgrims. Their clothes and blankets were wet and cold, and became stiff when the salt water dried. There was no fire to warm them or to dry their clothes. On very wet and cold days, a warm meal helped, when the Pilgrims could light a fire.

A storm at sea was very frightening for the Pilgrims.

When the seas were calm, some Pilgrims used fireboxes for boiling a stew or thick pea soup called pease pottage. In rough seas, there was a danger that the firebox could turn over and burn up the whole ship, so dinners often were eaten cold.

Biscuits and Salted Fish

The Pilgrims ate the same foods day after day for 66 days. Breakfast might have been a **ship's biscuit** and **moldy** cheese. Dinner was eaten at noon. The Pilgrims might have eaten pork or beef **jerky**, or salted fish, and a bit of cabbage, onion, or turnip. Spices such as cinnamon, ginger, and nutmeg helped to cover up the bad taste of rotting food. Supper was a small meal in the evening. Doughboys, small lumps of wet flour fried in pork fat, might have been eaten then. Burgoo, a hot oatmeal with molasses, or plum duff, a pudding with raisins and prunes, were other supper treats.

The Pilgrims didn't like to drink water on the Mayflower. It was unhealthy to drink the water carried on ships during those days. It was often dirty. Everyone drank beer with their meals, even the children.

The foods that the Pilgrims took with them on the Mayflower had to last for the whole voyage.

14

A Smelly Ship

The Mayflower started the trip smelling sweet like wine. Before long, it became a smelly ship. There was no bathtub and there was no extra water for washing clothes. The Pilgrims couldn't change their clothes. The items of clothing were packed away. Extra everyone wore the same clothes during the two-month voyage. There was no toilet, just a bucket in the corner that had to be dumped overboard once a day. When the passengers were seasick, they often vomited on themselves or their neighbors.

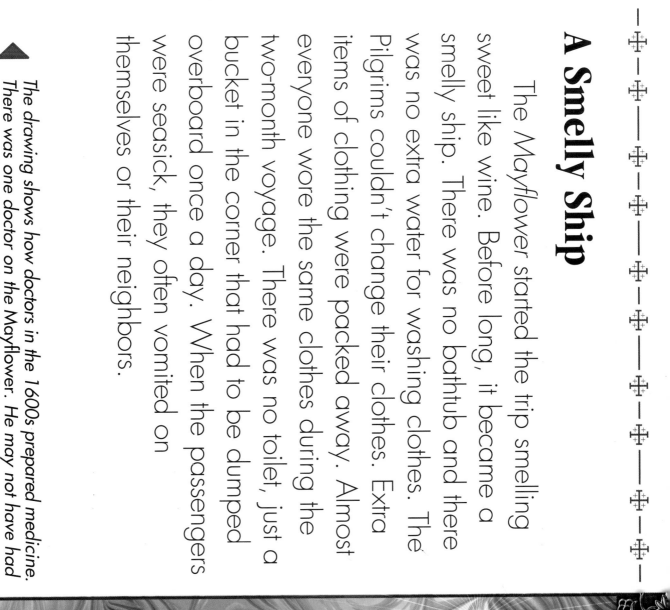

Will Butten, 23 years old, died of a fever and was buried at sea. Now there were only 101 Pilgrims on the Mayflower. Their numbers returned to 102 when Giles Hopkins's baby brother, Oceanus, was born during the Mayflower voyage.

▲ The drawing shows how doctors in the 1600s prepared medicine. There was one doctor on the Mayflower. He may not have had all the tools that he needed to help sick passengers.

Mayflower Passengers

The Pilgrims probably talked to Stephen Hopkins, Giles's father. He was the only one who had been to the New World. They looked to John Carver and William Bradford for leadership. Carver became their first governor after they settled in the New World. Bradford became the second governor. He later wrote a book about the Pilgrims' adventures. Miles Standish had been a soldier and could protect the Pilgrims when they got to the New World. There were also shopkeepers, a doctor, a **blacksmith**, and other tradesmen on the *Mayflower*.

Several tradesmen traveled on the Mayflower and settled in the New World.

There were so many people 'tween decks on the Mayflower that they had a hard time talking to each other. The children were forbidden to run. They had to play quiet games. They also could read the Bible. There were no children's books to read.

a weaver

workman's felt hat and shears for cutting cloth

a shoemaker

Sea Storms and Angry Sailors

The *Mayflower's* crew of 30 sailors called the Pilgrims "puke-stockings" because they were seasick and vomited so often. The sailors also thought the Saints sang and prayed too much. The Pilgrims thought the sailors used bad language. The sailors ended up being grateful for the Saints' prayers, however. The Pilgrims were grateful for the sailors' skills when the *Mayflower* sailed into storm after storm. The sky turned black, the winds screamed. The waves crashed into the tiny ship, and the cold, wet, sick Pilgrims huddled together in the dark.

▲ When the *Mayflower* was tossed by storms, the Pilgrims prayed that they would arrive in the New World safely.

On November 9, 1620, the Pilgrims were so happy when a sailor shouted "Land Ho!" William Bradford wrote, "Being brought safe to land, they fell upon their knees and blessed the God of Heaven who had brought them over the vast and furious ocean."

Landing in the New World

The Mayflower sailed into Cape Cod Bay, which would become part of the state of Massachusetts many years later. When the Pilgrims first saw Cape Cod, it was a **wilderness**, just a little beach and some trees. There were no houses, no shops, and no one to welcome them. Before anyone could get off the Mayflower and go ashore, there was an important decision to be made. If everyone went seperate ways, they all would surely die. Instead, the men wrote and signed the Mayflower Compact. In the Compact it was agreed that the Saints and Strangers would all stay together, work together, and make decisions together for the good of the community.

The Mayflower was a temporary home for the Pilgrims. It stayed in Cape Cod for six months. Then it sailed back to England in April 1621. Today some barns and houses in England are said to be made of timbers from the Mayflower.

Glossary

blacksmith (BLAK-smith) A person who makes tools out of iron.

decks (DEKS) Platforms or areas of a ship.

jerky (JUR-kee) Dried slices of meat.

moldy (MOL-dee) Covered with mold, fungus.

musket (MUS-kit) A gun with a long barrel used in battle and hunting.

Separatists (SEP-ah-rah-tists) People who belonged to a religious group that wanted to separate from the Church of England.

settlement (SEH-tul-ment) A small village or group of houses.

ship's biscuit (SHIPS BIS-kit) A hard, flat biscuit, about the size of a plate.

survive (sur-VYV) To stay alive.

timber (TIM-bur) Wood that is cut and used for building houses, ships, and other wooden objects.

tradesmen (TRAYDZ-min) People who are trained to do special work with their hands.

wilderness (WIL-dur-nis) An area that is wild and has no permanent settlement.

Index

A
America, 5, 6, 9

B
Bradford, William, 18

C
Cape Cod Bay, 22
Carver, John, 18
clothes, 17

E
England, 5

F
foods, 14

H
Hopkins, Elizabeth, 9
Hopkins, Giles, 9, 10
Hopkins, Stephen, 18

M
Massachusetts, 22
Mayflower Compact, 22

P
Plymouth, England, 5, 13
prayers, 21

S
Saints, 6, 21, 22
seasick, 17, 21
Separatists, 5
Speedwell, 6
Standish, Miles, 18
storm(s), 13, 21
Strangers, 22

T
tradesmen, 6, 18

W
wet, 13, 21

Web Sites

For more information about the Pilgrims and the Mayflower, check out these Web sites:
www.mayflower.org
www.pilgrims.net/plymouth

24